A Handbook for Outreach

Outreach

March 2001

Foreword

"Our mission is working with others to conserve, protect, and enhance fish, wildlife, and plants and their habitats for the continuing benefit of the American people."

One of the most important changes in the way the U.S. Fish and Wildlife Service accomplishes its mission is now reflected by three words at the beginning of our mission statement: "working with others." These words reflect our acknowledgement that we cannot effectively carry out our enormous natural resources management mission single-handedly. This Handbook for Outreach, with key guidance, policies, and helpful tips, will serve as your one-stop reference on how to enlist the support of a wide range of "others," i.e., our publics, by improving our communications with them.

How can Outreach help the Service do its job? As America continues to grow, natural resource management problems have become immensely complicated by the involvement of people from many different segments of the public. Successful resolution of these problems requires effective communication with these publics. To gain their support for our mission, it is imperative that we provide them a clear picture of the needs of fish and wildlife resources and the consequences of human intervention, be they positive or negative. Our success in this endeavor depends on how well the American people trust the U.S. Fish and Wildlife Service.

To be trusted by a skeptical public, an organization must not only perform well, but also be publicly appreciated for its good performance. Our science and judgment in managing natural resources are sound, and creditworthy. However, too many Americans do not even know who we are or what we do. As a result, we are often mistrusted, wrongly criticized, and many of those who would share our values work against us instead of with us. Effective outreach can help us gain the trust and assistance of our various publics, while providing us a mechanism to listen, and where appropriate, accommodate reasonable concerns.

Outreach is not just about making the Service "look good." It's about building trust. Outreach is a management tool to help us develop and maintain the trust and understanding of the American people. With their trust will come their support for us in our mission to conserve, protect, and enhance fish, wildlife and plants for their benefit.

Guide to Using the Outreach Handbook

This booklet is intended to serve as a one-stop, quick reference guide on Outreach, and to serve as your central location for:

- Step-by-step directions for preparing an Outreach Plan

- A practical overview of key components of good outreach

- Regulations, policies and directives regarding the practice of outreach.

- Suggestions and tips to help make your outreach effective and creative.

This booklet is designed so you can update it as needed. Feel free to customize it by adding articles, other outreach guidance, or your own material to keep it up to date.

The National Conservation Training Center offers training in all phases of outreach, both at the Center and in local areas. For information, check their website (www.fws.gov/r9nctc/nctc.html) or call 304-876-7200.

Acknowledgments

Much of the information in this Outreach Handbook draws upon the excellent outreach guidance that has been previously prepared by forward-looking Service employees from all Regions. The fact that specific material in this booklet has been incorporated from that guidance should be seen as the strongest possible endorsement of that fine work. Key publications excerpted in, or used in the preparation of the Outreach Handbook include the following:

Region 1:
"Regional Outreach Strategy," 1992
"Outreach Handbook"
"Field Guide to Outreach"

Region 5:
"One Step at a Time: An Outreach Handbook," 1995
"A Plan for Congressional Relations," 1998

Region 7:
"Region 7 Outreach Report," 1995

National Conservation Training Center:
Various publications and lesson plans.

Table of Contents

Appendices

  A-1 Approvals

    Guidance and Forms for outreach-related activities which require approval

    A-1 a. Approval form for Publications (DI-550)

    A-1 b. Approval form for Audio-Visual Production (DI-551)

    A-1 c. Approval for Special Events of National Significance (042 FW 1.1.6.A)

  A-2 National Outreach Strategy

  A-3 Planning Models

    A-3 a. Director's Memorandum, "Outreach Planning for Significant Decisions"

    A-3 b. Region 1 10-Step Model Process ("Field Guide to Outreach")

    A-3 c. Region 5 7-Step Model Process ("Region 5 Outreach Workbook")

    A-3 d. Region 7 7-Step Model Process ("Region 7 Outreach Checklist")

  A-4 Congressional Relations

    A-4 a. Reminder and Final Guidelines When Meeting with Members of Congress
           Director's Memorandum, April 1, 1999

    A-4 b. Congressional Meetings
           Memorandum from Assistant Director,
           External Affairs, February 23, 1998

Chapter 1: Introduction

Definition of Outreach:

Outreach is two-way communication between the U.S. Fish and Wildlife Service and the public to establish mutual understanding, promote involvement, and influence attitudes and actions, with the goal of improving joint stewardship of our natural resources. (From the National Outreach Strategy)

The Basics of Service Outreach

"It's About Building Trust"

The fundamental purpose of Service outreach is to build understanding and trust in the Service by helping members of various publics understand who we are, what we do, and why we do it. The *National Outreach Strategy* (See Appendix A-2) describes a Service-wide approach that brings consistency to outreach efforts by specifying unified messages and a unified approach for delivering those messages. All Service outreach— including yours—gains synergy through consistency. Your effective outreach conducted in harmony with other Service outreach at local, regional, and national levels will resonate in audiences, build on familiar themes, and form a much stronger impression than outreach conducted independently.

The Danger Zones of Outreach

How to do great outreach and stay out of trouble!

Outreach can be a powerful tool to help the Service carry out its mission. However, those involved in Outreach must insure that it is carried out in accordance with the guidance, regulations, and laws. Be sure to familiarize yourself with possible restrictions in these areas:

1. Lobbying.
Do not engage, discuss or relay any information that deals with pending federal legislation or appropriation without coordinating closely with your Congressional Liaison.
(See Chapter 3.a., Appendix A-4)

2. Copyright.
Do not use information materials taken or copied from private or commercial sources. This applies to photographs, film, and videotape productions, as well as publications. In some cases, permission may be granted, but find out how to obtain permission before you use copyrighted material.
(Consult with your Assistant Regional Director for External Affairs, or the Departmental Office of the Solicitor)

3. Libel, Slander.
Do not publicly criticize individuals, organizations, or businesses. Stick to the Service's key messages, and you won't have any problems here.

4. Accessibility for Citizens with Disabilities.
When planning for any outreach or information program, including exhibits and special events, remember to take into consideration citizens with various disabilities.
(Consult with your Assistant Regional Director for Human Resources)

5. Surveys.
Surveys are an excellent way to obtain information about the public, but *formal surveys of the public may not be conducted without obtaining approval from the Office of Management and Budget.* Outreach may draw upon results of surveys already independently conducted by others. *(See Chapter 3)* *(Consult with your Assistant Regional Director for External Affairs)*

6. Approvals.
Remember that many Outreach products and activities require either written approvals from, or coordination with, specific offices. Examples include:

a. Publications. In addition to being approved in advance, publications should conform to Service Graphic Standards.

b. Audio-visual productions.

c. Exhibits.

d. New web pages. (Updating information already posted does not require approval)

e. Special events that involve high level officials, or those that focus on highly visible (or controversial) issues.

f. Advertising. Use of appropriated funds for commercial advertising (unless specifically authorized) is prohibited.

Plan your outreach early to find out about and obtain needed approvals.

For details on required approvals, see relevant chapters, Appendix A-1, or consult with your Assistant Regional Director for External Affairs.

Components of an Outreach Plan

Outreach gains synergy through consistency

Just like most other endeavors, effective outreach benefits must be well planned. This handbook provides guidance on how to prepare a plan to make your outreach more effective and consistent with other Service outreach. At any given point in your outreach activity, check to be sure that your outreach plan and efforts follow these guidelines:

I. Goals of Service Outreach.

When it is effectively carried out, Service outreach will:

- Make it easier for employees to carry out their natural resource management responsibilities.

- Improve support for the agency's mission.

- Build new partnerships

- Improve service to the public

- Strengthen the credibility and stature of the Service.

Test: What are the goals of the project or program you are conducting? How do they correspond with and reinforce Service outreach goals?

Key Point: Outreach for your project should support the goals of your project or program specifically, while reinforcing the national goals generally. In other words, the communication goal of your outreach should be to focus attention on the *outcome* of the Service management activity, and *not just the process* of the management activity.

(See "National Outreach Strategy," Appendix A-2)

II. Service Publics.

Outreach efforts should consider establishing communication with all potentially interested publics, always with an emphasis on reaching the *decision-makers and opinion leaders* of each group. Specific "key" publics you should consider including are groups or individuals who have commented on previous Service actions.

Test: Do your outreach efforts include each of those groups that could be most affected by, or interested in your project or program?

Key Point: Effective outreach must target specific, key publics, and should consider including those with a record of interest in Service issues. Recurring outreach with the same publics builds Service identity and trust.

(See Chapter 2.a. "Service Publics," and Chapter 3 "Special Audiences")

III. Service Messages.

For members of disparate publics to understand and remember them, our messages should be kept simple and be repeated. These messages help explain how our work relates to the public's areas of greatest concern. All Service programs and activities can be explained using one or more of the following messages:

- The U.S. Fish and Wildlife Service is a Federal agency whose mission, working with others, is to conserve fish, wildlife, plants and their habitats.

- The Service helps protect a healthy environment for people, fish and wildlife.

- The Service helps Americans conserve and enjoy the outdoors.

Test: Are ALL of our outreach efforts conveying and reinforcing these messages?

Key Point: In order to get through, messages must be simple and repeated, using the same language.

(See Chapter 2.b., "Messages")

IV. Evaluation.

Effective outreach that helps the Service can be documented, and can be quantified in two ways:

Products — Products are what you produce and distribute to support your outreach to deliver your message. Measure them by keeping a detailed list of what products you produce, how many, and documenting when and where they are used.

Results — Results should be determined by obtaining feedback from the targeted publics to determine whether they are getting the outreach message, and if applicable, changing behavior or attitudes because of the outreach. The evaluation phase of outreach planning should include a process for obtaining this feedback.

Test: Does the outreach being conducted include a mechanism for obtaining feedback?

Key Point: Use feedback to find out whether the targeted publics are getting the message. The process of seeking feedback helps build buy-in and trust.

(See Appendix A-3 for suggestions on how to evaluate outreach)

Chapter 2: Preparing the Outreach Plan

Why Use the Outreach Plan?

The outreach planning model in this handbook closely resembles or corresponds with the models currently being used by the most successful organizations in the world, including the major national and international public relations firms. They use it because it works—not just to look good, but to help accomplish their organizational goals.

- Outreach planning is a management tool. It requires involvement and buy in of managers whose continuing support is required to make it happen.

- Outreach planning helps set priorities, and ultimately saves time, money, and the resource.

- Outreach Plans are now *required* for all the Service's "significant decisions." Such decisions can include, but are not limited to: Endangered Species Act listings, high-profile recovery plans, species reintroductions, land acquisitions, migratory bird or predator control actions, public access to outdoor recreation, contaminant issues with human health concerns, major Natural Resource Damage Assessment settlements, major scientific findings on the status of a species or an ecosystem, or actions involving large expenditures of funds. (See Appendix A-3.a.)

Guidance from several Regions, the National Outreach Strategy, and the Director's Memorandum "Outreach Plans for Significant Decisions" each have excellent directions on how to prepare comprehensive, effective outreach plans. The Region 1 Outreach Handbook describes a process for building a "Communications Platform" as a "blueprint for action." Region 5 takes a similar step-by-step approach with its "Outreach Workbook," and the Region 7 Outreach Report features an "Outreach Checklist Worksheet." The Region 4 Communications Model defines five "channels" of communication in outreach efforts.

Each of these models emphasizes a comprehensive, collaborative approach to outreach. They each lay out a process to produce an effective, economic, and accountable plan of outreach activities bound by unity of purpose and message. Though individual steps differ slightly between models, the end result is the same: A focused effort conducted throughout the life of a program or project to generate understanding, trust, and support from a variety of groups. This support will have a direct bearing on the Service's ability to successfully accomplish its projects or activities.

Planning is accomplished best by a small group of people that may include project leaders, subject matter experts, and sometimes even partner organizations. A facilitator skilled in outreach planning should lead the group through the process

The model in this chapter is taken from the one provided in the National Outreach Strategy (Appendix 2). Since each Service issue that requires an outreach plan is new and different, planners are encouraged to adopt elements from other outreach models as needed. Sample forms and references to other guidance with helpful tips are also included in this section and in appendices.

Outreach Planning Model

The main purpose for an outreach plan is to insure that the efforts you put into outreach really do help achieve the Service's resource management objectives. A good outreach plan should be brief and to the point. The following Outreach Planning Model identifies the eight basic components which should be included in each outreach plan:

Assessment:
- State the problem, issue or situation, and why action is necessary in one or two clear, concise sentences. The statement should be simple and direct to keep everyone focused.

- Identify those who may be affected by the problem, issue or situation.

- Briefly describe how the current problem, issue or situation affects fish and wildlife resources, and specifically the Service's ability to accomplish its objectives in resource management.

Audiences(s):
- Which publics (individuals or groups) can we reach who will have the most influence on the outcome of the issue?

- What are the concerns, expectations, perceptions and biases of each of these publics?

- Describe each target audience in one concise sentence.

- List the key "Internal Publics": Service and Department Officials who should be informed of the issue or situation BEFORE you begin the outreach.

- List all Congressional delegation officials, and other Federal, state, county or city officials who need to be contacted about the issue.

- List local, regional, and (if appropriate) national level news media who may be likely to cover the issue.

- List specific constituent and interest groups who may become involved and should be contacted (See Chapters 2.a., 3).

Goal:
- What is the desired outcome of the issue or situation?

- What do we want members of the identified publics to think, feel, or do (or not do), as a result of the outreach on the issue?

- State the outreach goal in one clear concise sentence.

Message:
- What do we want our audiences to know or understand?

- How can we use the Service's three basic messages to explain why this issue is important to people as well as to wildlife?

- State the main message in one clear concise sentence.

Tools:
- What outreach tools are most appropriate to achieving our goal?

- Which tools are most appropriate to convey the message to each audience?

- List each tool to be used in the entire outreach effort.

Schedule:
- Are there specific dates (such as publication of a Federal Register Notice, or other deadlines) that this issue or situation is tied to?

- List the specific outreach activities needed for this issue (for example, briefings of officials, public meetings, press releases and press conferences, development and distribution of mailings or posters, etc.).

- Develop a schedule or time line that shows when each of these activities must occur.

Implementation:
- What personnel, funds, and supplies are needed to implement this outreach effort?

- What internal and external partners can be involved in the outreach effort?

- What resources will we provide, and what resources will partners provide?

- List a budget for the entire outreach effort.

Reality Check:
- Does every item listed in your Outreach Plan contribute to achieving the resource management goal? Can any item be improved upon?

- Identify a method that will be used to evaluate the effectiveness of each step in the schedule after it has been carried out. Be prepared to use the evaluation to revise the plan accordingly.

You are now ready to carry out effective outreach in support of the Service's resource-management goals and objectives!

(For detailed guidance and suggestions on how to carry out each of these steps, see Appendix A-3.)

Sample Outreach Plan Format

This sample format (which is included in the National Outreach Strategy) should be used for documents requiring outreach plans. This format may be adapted or modified as needed, as long as the information covered here is included.

Title
(Outreach Plan for the _____)

Issue:
(State issue in one or two sentences.)

Basic Facts about the Issue:
(In bullets or *short* paragraphs, outline basic facts about the action and why it is needed.)

Communication Goals:
(In a few bullets, state what you want to see as the outcome of your communications effort. If appropriate, address how the action will affect people and include what the Service will do to address public concerns.)

Message:
(In one short sentence, state why this issue is important to people and wildlife. Whenever possible, say how the action contributes to a healthy, clean environment; to outdoor recreation; or to preservation of important American heritage and traditions.)

Interested Parties:
(Identify groups/individuals who will be most affected or are otherwise interested in this action)

Key Date:
(If there is a specific date the action is tied to, such as a court action or Federal Register publication, fill it in.)

Strategy:
(Explain your strategy for communicating this information. For example, do you plan to hold a press conference, accompanied by in-person briefings for concerned groups? Can the information be communicated simply by news release, or perhaps only phone calls to key people are required?)

Action Plan:
- (Under "Interested Party," list who needs to be contacted. Include Members of Congress or their staffs; State and local officials; news reporters; business/agricultural leaders; and constituent groups. Include groups who disagree as well as those who support the action.)
- (Under "Method of Contact," indicate whether the person will be contacted by phone, personal meeting, briefing, etc.)
- (Under "Person Responsible," indicate what FWS employee or cooperator will make the contact.)
- (Under "Phone/Fax," list appropriate numbers so you will have them handy.)
- (Under "Date," list date when contact is to be made.)

Action Plan

Interested Party	Method of Contact	Person Responsible	Phone/Fax	Date

The National Conservation Training Center offers training on this subject and all phases of outreach, both at the Center and in local areas. For information, check their website (www.fws.gov/r9nctc/nctc.html) or call 304-876-7200

The more narrowly defined the specific public is, the easier it is to determine HOW to communicate with them.

Summary: Why should the Service focus its outreach efforts on various, specific publics? For one thing, America has always drawn its strength from its diversity of ideas. Because of this diversity, there is no single public, but rather a great many separate publics that are determined by each specific issue at hand. The bottom line is that many different publics can have a significant bearing on how or whether the Service accomplishes its mission. The primary advantages of identifying specific publics are:

1. The more narrowly defined the target public is, the easier it is to determine HOW to communicate with them, and the more effective the outreach effort will be.

2. Preparing a check list in advance of key publics helps to ensure that outreach planning does not inadvertently overlook a group that could have a stake in a Service program or project.

Key Publics

Various Service outreach teams, such as the Refuges Outreach Team, and Regional Outreach Teams, have identified key publics as a checklist for their outreach activities. Below are these categories of publics and some of the reasons why they are important to include in outreach:

Congress—Delegation and staff members.
Why? All of the Service publics are constituents of Congress. Good communication with Congress is essential for a federal agency to be effective and responsive to the American public.

Conservation Groups.
Why? They have great interest in resource management, and their support or lack of it influences other publics

Corporations—The businesses community, large and small.
Why? They often communicate economic impacts of resource management decisions, good or bad; can influence Congress; can be a source of funding or moral support through partnerships.

Communities.
Why? They can be directly impacted by Service activities; can directly impact fish and wildlife resources; can influence Congress.

Communications (News Media, etc.)
Why? They can directly influence virtually all other publics.

U.S. Fish and Wildlife Service ("in-reach")
Why? They are essential for internal support and to help communicate messages.

Other Federal Agencies
Why? Their objections can block Service activities; support enhances Service credibility, gives momentum to Service initiatives.

State and Local Government
Why? Their objections can erode other publics' confidence or directly block Service activities. Their support can enhance a project's likelihood of success.

Educational Institutions/Programs
Why? Students adopt long-term values regarding environmental stewardship. Student and faculty opinions can either enhance or erode Service credibility.

Special interest groups.
Why? They represent and communicate directly with many specialized publics; can influence other publics, including Congress.

Native Americans
Why? They have direct interests in fish and wildlife resources through their subsistence, traditions and

spirituality; unique organizational status and relationship with Federal government; control of large areas of land.

Resource users
Why? These groups are well defined by their common interests (hunters, birders, anglers, etc.) and often are directly affected by Service activities and decisions. They can have direct impact on resources; can gain sympathy from or exert influence on otherwise unaffected publics, including Congress.

Other publics?
As you plan outreach for each program or project, do not hesitate to "think outside the box" when identifying important publics. Each new situation is different, and communities and cultures are forever evolving. Watch for opportunities to reach out to new interest groups and non-traditional publics who could support the Service mission.

How to Identify, Work with Key Publics for Your Outreach Plan

Warning: Do NOT try this Alone!

- Determine your key publics for your outreach plan:

a. Use a *group* of co-workers involved in your project to help. Most of the publics will be obvious, but those not considered adequately often cause the most problems. Your group dynamic will help identify key publics.

b. Then, go *outside* of the Service to ask partners who should be included.

c. Do not overlook *friends*— partners, employees. They can help communicate to other publics, and may feel betrayed by not getting the word on important issues. Do not risk losing their support!

d. Prioritize your publics, so that you can place your resources where they will do the most good. Before you finalize your list, consider the resources available to do your outreach, and keep it realistic.

e. *Remember to always include the U.S. Fish and Wildlife Service—your chain of command and fellow employees—as a key public. Since they, too, are the Service, it helps them all to know what the Service is saying to everyone else!*

■ Learn about your publics. Once you select each public, determine what they know about the issue:

a. What are their positions on the issue?

b. What is the best way to communicate with them?

How do you answer these questions? A formal survey would help, but you do not need a complicated, scientifically precise survey to get a good idea:

a. *Ask their leaders;*

b. Or, establish and ask one or more "key informants," individual contacts you know and trust who are members of the particular public. Ask your contact to take the pulse of their group and tell you frankly what they think;

c. Or, as a minimum, informally ask several random members (2-6) of these publics.

Communicate with these contacts *before, during and after* your outreach efforts. Record the feedback for your evaluation!

Two excellent processes for identifying and analyzing outreach audiences have been developed by Region 1 and Region 5. See Appendix A-3

Getting to Know Your Publics:

What Do Americans Think about Government and Environmental Issues?

When communicating the Service messages, it helps to know something about attitudes of the American public in general to anticipate how messages will be received. The following research, taken from national surveys in recent years, may be helpful in crafting your outreach messages.

According to a December 1998 survey of adult Americans conducted by Roper Starch Worldwide for the National Environmental Education and Training Foundation (NEETF):

■ More than 60 percent believe the economy and environment can go hand in hand.

■ If they had to choose, 70 percent would choose environment over economy.

■ Less than 20 percent believe regulation has gone too far.

■ More than 45 percent believe regulation has not gone far enough.

Among the study's conclusions:

■ Americans are concerned about the environment and generally want the government to be actively involved in its protection.

■ What may be especially alarming is the widespread and persistent nature of the misinformation among most demographic subgroups. (56% of Americans believe that six-pack rings are the main cause of fish and wildlife entanglement. However, the main cause is abandoned fishing line left by anglers, a fact known by only 10%)

■ There is a need to provide environmental information in a form that the American public can more easily remember and internalize.

■ The responsibility for moving in the direction of greater information and understanding rests with public agencies, non-governmental organizations, the environmental community, and the media.

An April 1996 Survey by Beldon and Russonello Research, conducted for the Consultative Group on Biological Diversity, reported that Americans support environmental protections for the following reasons:

■ Wanting one's family to live in a healthy, pleasing environment (79%).

■ Responsibility to leave the earth in good shape for future generations (71%).

■ Appreciation for beauty of nature (63%).

■ Belief that "all life found in nature has a right to exist" (55%).

What should the Service's role in environmental issues be?

Do Americans hate the federal government? Are they receptive to federal agencies taking an active role in public matters? A June 1998 national survey by the Pew Center for the People and the Press asked whether Americans wanted an "active Federal government." According to the survey results:

■ Only 28% of federal employees believe that Americans are "pro-government."

■ 33% of members of Congress believe that Americans are "pro-government."

But in reality, the survey found:

■ 57% of Americans say they are "pro-government."

Other Useful Survey Results

Survey results from various sources are also available, including "Wildlife and the American Mind: Public Opinion and Attitudes toward Fish and Wildlife Management," 1998, by Mark D. Duda, et al., Responsive Management National Office, Harrisonburg, VA 22801 (www.responsivemanagement.com)

Type of Public vs. Type of Communication

The individual characteristics of each public help determine the best strategies for communicating with that public.

Examples:

■ Most special and public interest groups (environmental groups, outdoor recreation groups, etc.) have internal newsletters whose editors may use written materials; they often have regular membership meetings where oral presentations may be made.

■ Congressional members and their staffs get most information from personal briefings, succinct briefing statements, formal reports, Federal Register, etc.

■ Businesses and industry leaders get information from trade journals and other specialized media.

■ Students get information through school lesson plans from teachers, and from specialized classroom publications, like "Weekly Reader," "Scholastic," and "Science World."

As you consider each organized public, make a point to find out how that organization communicates with its members and use their media. If it is an unorganized public, try to determine specific media that its members use to get information about the interests that unite them.

The *News Media* are a special case, in that they are both a public and a strategy to get information to other publics.

■ As a *public*, members of the news media get their information through:

a. Personal contact (phone calls, visits)

b. Press releases (by fax, mail, hand carried, etc.)

c. Internet web sites and e-mail.

(Note: According to a 1999 survey by Global Financial Communication Network, 60% of reporters prefer news releases to be sent by FAX instead of e-mail. Ask your reporters their preferences!)

■ As a *strategy*, news media help to provide information to virtually all other publics, but remember:

a. News media are *good* for raising awareness about an issue among many publics.

b. News media are *not good* for conveying complex information on a controversial issue.

(See Chapter 3.b., "Media Relations")

Making Contact, Achieving Success with Your Publics

Make it Personal!

For every public, gaining trust and support begins with building relationships and establishing credibility. In a comprehensive outreach plan, many methods are used to help raise awareness, allay fears and generate involvement. But when it comes to gaining trust and effective support, in the end there is no substitute for personal relationships with the *decision-makers and opinion leaders* for each specific public.

When public issues become controversial and generate conflict between opposing groups (including the Service), public relations professionals (e.g., Jackson, Jackson & Wagner) have crafted effective communications based on the following theory of public opinion and conflict resolution:

1. Whatever one side says, the other side has data that refute it. Facts seem to matter less and less and truth becomes irrelevant in the public debate. Solid, simple information must be boldly presented in a way that grabs attention. Even then, *skepticism reigns*. Information from mass media tends to reinforce old opinions rather than stimulate new opinions.

2. In an atmosphere of conflict, people form opinions based on hearsay. Interpersonal, word-of-mouth, face-to-face programs are vital because *credibility shifts* from the information carried by mass media to the information carried by individuals whom people trust.

3. Communications that *focus on the solution*, not the problem, gain more attention and support. Emphasis shifts from the conflicting data to solving the problem.

4. Success depends on existing relationships with opinion leaders and decision-makers. Even if they do not have a direct stake in the outcome, these individuals become trusted, *third-party advocates* for "the solution," and generate support from those publics they represent.

Many Service leaders and individuals have learned that they can, and must, build those relationships *in person*. They make frequent personal visits with organizational opinion leaders and decision-makers and give presentations to local organizations. When they become personally involved with organizations and community activities, members of various publics can get to know and trust them as individuals and members of the community—not just "the feds." They are seen as qualified and dedicated professionals who are capable of making resource management decisions in the best interests of the community they live in themselves.

Chapter 2.b.: Service Messages

Summary: In order to build trust and support among its many publics across the nation, the Service must not only perform its mission well, but also gain recognition from those publics. This process begins by insuring that all those publics understand first of all who we are, what we do, and why we do it. The Service's basic messages will help Americans gain this understanding.

Antidote to Infoglut: Simplicity, Repetition

Why should all Service outreach use the same messages? Thanks in part to advances in information technology, Americans today are bombarded by information in a non-stop process that has been called "infoglut." Like the Service, thousands of other organizations compete for Americans' attention. Big businesses spend billions of dollars globally simply to gain and retain name recognition, because they know that in order for the public to trust their brand name, the public must first recognize their brand name. In this highly competitive atmosphere, the only messages to get through are those that are simple and repeated.

By repeating the same messages in all its activities, Service Outreach gains synergy through consistency. All Service programs and activities can be explained using one or more of the following messages:

1. The U.S. Fish and Wildlife Service is a Federal agency whose mission, working with others, is to conserve fish, wildlife, plants and their habitats.

2. The Service helps protect a healthy environment for people, fish and wildlife.

3. The Service helps Americans conserve and enjoy the outdoors.

Crafting the Convergence: Service Messages — Your Project's Messages

Warning: Do NOT try this Alone!

During your outreach planning phase, use your best creative abilities, along with those of your co-workers and partners, to craft the message which best captures the Service messages AND those of the immediate project or activity at hand. As you refine your messages, keep these points in mind:

- Repetition: The more closely the message captures the meanings of the Service's basic messages, the more synergy it will have with other Service outreach activities.

- Simplicity: Can your messages be conveyed in one or two "sound bites"? Can it easily be incorporated into a presentation, a fact sheet, a public service announcement (PSA), or an exhibit?

Be sure to TEST your message statements on a sample of people from target publics to ensure that the messages can be easily understood.

For more ideas and tips on crafting your outreach messages, see Appendix A-3

Chapter 3: Special Audiences
Chapter 3.a.: Congressional Relations

Summary: As one of the Service's most important audiences, members of Congress and their staffs require specialized procedures for communicating important issues effectively. The term "Congress" encompasses members of the U.S. House of Representatives and the U.S. Senate, and members of their staffs, both in Washington D.C. and in their home states or districts. As an important Service public, all Service outreach should consider including Congress in the communications process.

Key Contacts for Congressional Relations:

Regional Congressional Liaison: _____ Phone: _____ Fax: _____

    E-mail: _____ Address: _____

U.S. Senator (Senior): _____ Phone: _____ Fax: _____

    E-mail: _____ Addresses (Local/D.C.) _____

    Key Staff members, D.C.:

    Key Staff members, local:

U.S. Senator (Junior): _____ Phone: _____ Fax: _____

    E-mail: _____ Address: (Local/D.C.) _____

    Key Staff members, D.C.:

    Key Staff members, local:

District Representative to U.S. House: _____ Phone: _____ Fax: _____

    E-mail: _____ Address: (Local/D.C.) _____

    Key Staff members, D.C.:

    Key Staff members, local:

Dealing with Members of Congress and Their Staffs:

Be Proactive, but Be Prudent!

In the past, the Service's Congressional Relations activities tended to be very issue-specific, often with the Service reacting to direct questions from members of Congress or their staffs. In November 1997, the Director issued a memo to encourage Service employees to take a more proactive approach to congressional relations by initiating contacts with congressional Members and staff.

To make the most of these contacts, they should be carefully planned following the principles and procedures of outreach applicable to other Service audiences.

1. The *Goals* of outreach to Congress remain the same as the goals for all other outreach: To build understanding and trust in the Service by strengthening its stature and credibility, ultimately resulting in benefits to the natural resources under Service stewardship.

2. The *Basic Service Messages remain the same* for outreach to Congress as for all other outreach. Be sure to reinforce the Service's basic messages as you provide information on specific issues of interest.

3. *Advise your Regional Congressional Liaison* of ALL contacts you initiate or receive from Members of Congress or their staff. Your liaison can offer assistance and advise you of other issues of sensitivity you should understand prior to your contact.

Note: Prior to initiating contacts with Members or their staffs, be sure you are familiar with Regional policies for Congressional Relations. Contact your Regional Congressional Liaison for details.

Cautions on Lobbying

In all communications activities involving Congress, be sure you understand the federal laws that prohibit federal employees from "lobbying":

- *18 U.S.C. Section 1913* prohibits the use of appropriated funds for activities that directly or indirectly are "intended or designed to influence in any manner a Member of Congress, to favor or oppose" any legislation or appropriation by Congress.

- *Recent Interior Appropriations Acts* prohibit the use of appropriated funds for "any activity or the publication or distribution of literature that in any way tends to promote public support or opposition to any legislative proposal on which congressional action is not complete."

In one recent case, a Service employee was invited by a non-governmental organization to speak at a press conference called to generate opposition to pending legislation. It was determined that remarks the employee made at the press conference "tended to promote public opposition to the legislative proposal and hence violated the restriction."

Contact your Regional Congressional Liaison (or, if at Headquarters, the Office of Congressional and Legislative Affairs) for guidance if you have any doubts as to the applicability of these prohibitions on an action or activity you are considering.

See Appendix A-4 for detailed guidance and additional information on lobbying.

Maximizing your Effectiveness with Elected Officials

While there are many ways to communicate with elected officials and their staff, meeting face-to-face provides an extremely effective way to convey information. Meetings should first be scheduled with local district office staff to introduce yourself and discuss your responsibilities within the Fish and Wildlife Service. Refuge or field station visits provide an ideal setting for such meetings. Many staff look forward to getting out of their offices and away from phones, e-mail, and interruptions as much as we do. Give them the opportunity!!!! Before you do schedule a meeting, be prepared. Identify the message you want the staffer, Representative or Senator to take home. Begin with the end in mind. If they're asking for a meeting, do your homework. Research the issue and go prepared.

The following steps can provide guidance in preparing for a Congressional visit.

SETTING UP A MEETING

Plan Ahead
Whether you want to meet with a staff person or the Congressman, you will need an advance appointment. Phone or write well ahead of time, particularly if you want to meet with the Congressman. The District office staff generally schedule the Congressman's time while he is in the District, and a scheduler or appointments secretary while they are in Washington. Due to the press of time, the Congressman may not be able to see you even if you request a meeting with them rather than staff. Do not express any disappointment if this occurs; if you have a message to communicate, it should go to whomever they designate to meet with you. If you have already established regular contact with the staff, it will be much easier for you to get a meeting with the Congressman.

Determine whether the meeting should be in the District or in Washington. Generally, you will have a much better chance of meeting with the Congressman, and of spending more time with them, when they are in the District, while in DC you are more likely to get a short meeting with the staff. The Regional Congressional Liaison can be very helpful in deciding where to hold the meeting. Any meeting you hold with a Congressman or staff in Washington MUST be reported to the Regional Congressional Liaison person, no later than Thursday of the preceding week, for coordination purposes.

Create an Agenda
Know what you want to discuss. If appropriate, provide an agenda with room to write notes. This can prompt questions from the staffer or Congressman.

Keep the Meeting Short and with the Proper Level of Scientific Detail
If you are meeting with the Congressman or staff at their office, either Washington or DC, indicate how much time you will need when you request the appointment. Generally, you should ask for 15 or 30 minutes—less than 15 minutes indicates the issue is not substantial enough for them to hear you (unless it is a "courtesy/just stop by to say hello" visit, in which case indicate this), and more than 30 minutes is probably more time than they have for any one issue. If, on the other hand, you have the opportunity to have the staff or Congressman tour your facility the meeting will obviously be longer. Don't show more examples of the same issues in different area of a refuge. *IMPORTANT:* Start at the most basic level. Some staff may know all of the jargon from the Endangered Species Act. Most do not.

Know your Representative and Senators
Remember that the Representative and/or Senator represents all of their constituents. That doesn't mean they agree with all of the constituents. Learn the political background of the elected officials. Read the newspapers to understand where the Representative or Senator is coming from. Your Regional External Affairs Office through its Legislative Liaison, can help you with this task.

Do your Homework
Legislators work on many complex issues and cannot be expected to be experts in all of them. Again remember to start you discussions at a basic level.

CONDUCTING THE MEETING

Start off on the Right Foot
BE ON TIME. Thank the Representative or Senator for taking the time from their busy schedule to meet with you. Offer the agenda, if appropriate. Note: if the meeting consists of touring a facility, have refreshments available. If you are away from any place to have a lunch, provide sandwiches, drinks, etc. DO NOT USE APPROPRIATED FUNDS TO PURCHASE REFRESHMENTS.

Keep it Simple, Concise and Brief
Don't get bogged down with details and jargon. Localize the issue by providing information on which constituents support your facility or action and why. Give names of those who support actions.

Maintain your Credibility
Never speculate, generalize, or guess. If you are unsure of an answer to a legislator's question, it is appropriate to say, "I don't know." Offer to follow up with a response. Credibility is the currency of an effective relationship.

Address Opposition
If you are contemplating an action that will have a negative effect on some constituents, be aware of who those constituents are and what their concerns are. Develop answers to those concerns before the meeting and briefly share both the anticipated concerns and your answers with the Congressman or staff. You will lose considerable credibility if you do not alert them to possible adverse public reactions to what you are discussing.

Provide Resources and Leave Summary Information
Before you, the elected official, or their staff leave, make sure all of the concerns of the elected official have been answered (or gotten back with). Leave a ONE page briefing statement reiterating the highlights of the purpose of the meeting.

FOLLOW UP ON THE MEETING

Maintain the Relationship
It's much easier to build an existing relationship than to develop one during rough times. Add elected officials and their staff to your mailing list for relevant reports. Call at least once every three months even if it's just to check in. Invite them to special events and photo opportunities at your facility.

Look to the Future and Hold No Grudges
Be tolerant of differences of opinion. There will always be another instance where each of you will need support in the future. Always show your appreciation for the legislator's or staff's willingness to meet with you.

In sum, plan ahead, know your issues and who is affected by your issues, and know your elected officials. This applies to state, county, and local officials.

Steps to Establish Congressional Relationships

- Identify and establish contact with members and staffers.

- Establish and maintain a process for keeping them informed.

- Invite them to visit your field station or office.

- Look ahead to special occasions. Invite lawmakers and staff individually and collectively to attend and participate.

- Do not at any point refer to a staff person as an "aide". They have titles, such as "District Representative" or "Legislative Assistant"; if that is too formal refer to "Jane Doe of Representative Smith's staff".

When Briefing Elected Officials:

- Use concrete examples to make your point

- Do not offer your personal opinion

- Be concise

- Be specific and practical

- Offer to help

- Leave a summary sheet

How to Maintain Contact:

- Phone calls

- Letters and Faxes

- Forward information on a regular basis

- Forward photos and news clippings of news events

- Repeat PERSONAL contacts with lawmakers and staff

- Ask the lawmakers and staff for their assistance!

- Highlight your lawmaker's assistance. Do NOT mention staff in press releases or other communications intended to reach the public; credit the lawmaker even if the staff did all the work. You should, however, thank the staff person privately, and consider other steps if appropriate, such as asking your ARD or Regional Director to write a "thank you" note to the staffer.

For more information and hints on Congressional Relations, See Appendix A-4

All persons who interact with Congressional Members or their staffs are encouraged to take advantage of specialized training offered by the National Conservation and Training Center (NCTC).

Chapter 3.b.: News Media Relations

Summary: The term "News Media" encompasses the print medium, including your local newspapers, and the broadcast medium, including your nearest television and radio stations most likely to carry news about your activity. The news media are the most economical way to raise awareness of an issue with the most people.

News Media are in Business

News is a commodity:

- To be valuable, information must be *accurate*. Inaccurate information is worthless, and ultimately harmful to the business.

- To be valuable, information must be *current*. If it's old, it isn't news.

- To be a dependable source of information to the public, most news organizations operate on regularly scheduled editions or broadcasts, and therefore all work under the constant pressure of *deadlines*.

- The News business generates its income from *advertisers*, who are interested in the size of the audience—the ratings—the news operation can generate. The quest for ratings tends to favor news coverage that is sensational, dramatic, conflict-oriented.

News Media and Outreach

The *News Media* are of particular importance to outreach activities, in that they are both a *public* and a *strategy* to get information to other publics.

- *Public:* As one of the Service's most important audiences, members of the news media require specialized procedures for communicating important issues effectively. Each news media outlet has a decision-maker, usually an editor or a reporter, who decides what news will be carried in each edition or broadcast. Members of the news media get their information through:

  a. press releases (by fax, e-mail, delivery, press conferences/ briefings)

  b. personal contact (phone calls, visits, press conferences/ briefings)

  c. Internet web sites, and other general reference sources.

(Note: According to a 1999 survey by Global Financial Communication Network, 60% of reporters prefer news releases to be sent by FAX. Ask your reporters their preferences!)

- *Strategy*: The news media is just one of many strategies to provide information to the public. It is the most effective strategy to provide information to the most people for the least cost, since virtually anyone who reads the newspapers, listens to radio, or watches television can be reached through the news media. However:

  a. News media is *very good* for raising awareness about an issue among many publics.

  b. News media is *not so good* for conveying complex information on a controversial issue.

For assistance in any news media activities, be sure to keep in contact with your Regional Media Relations Liaison or specified Outreach Coordinator, located in your Regional External Affairs Office. Please fill out the following and keep the completed form in this handbook up-to-date for quick reference:

Key Contacts for News Media

Regional Media Relations Liaison: _____ Phone: _____ Fax: _____

   E-mail: _____ Address: _____

(Note for reporters below, highlight each one's preferred method of contact)

Newspaper: _____ Addresses _____

   Reporter _____ Phone: _____ Fax: _____ E-mail: _____

   Reporter _____ Phone: _____ Fax: _____ E-mail: _____

TV News Station _____ Network affiliation? _____ Addresses _____

   Reporter _____ Phone: _____ Fax: _____ E-mail: _____

   Reporter _____ Phone: _____ Fax: _____ E-mail: _____

TV News Station _____ Network affiliation? _____ Addresses _____

   Reporter _____ Phone: _____ Fax: _____ E-mail: _____

   Reporter _____ Phone: _____ Fax: _____ E-mail: _____

TV News Station _____ Network affiliation? _____ Addresses _____

   Reporter _____ Phone: _____ Fax: _____ E-mail: _____

   Reporter _____ Phone: _____ Fax: _____ E-mail: _____

Radio Station _____ Network affiliation? _____ Addresses _____

   Reporter _____ Phone: _____ Fax: _____ E-mail: _____

Radio Station _____ Network affiliation? _____ Addresses _____

   Reporter _____ Phone: _____ Fax: _____ E-mail: _____

Others:

   Reporter/Org. _____ Phone: _____ Fax: _____ E-mail: _____

Duplicate as needed

Press Query Sheet

Date of Call/Contact: _____

Reporter's Name: _____ Organization: _____

Phone/Fax /e-mail: _____

Questions: _____

_____

_____

_____

Response: _____

_____

_____

_____

Query Referred to/Coordinated with: _____

_____

_____

_____

Anticipated Publication/Broadcast Date: _____

_____

_____

_____

Follow-up: _____

_____

_____

_____

Notes: _____

_____

_____

_____

Your Local Office Policy for Press Calls

All staff members should understand office policy for taking calls from the news media. The project leader should set policies for each office and should identify those who are capable of and comfortable with serving as official Service spokespersons for the office. The following guidance applies to all Service press relations:

- All calls from news reporters should be taken immediately, or returned ASAP by someone who has been designated to serve as an official Service spokesperson.

- The spokesperson should comment on or explain issues *within the scope and responsibility of their project or activities.*

- The spokesperson DOES NOT NEED to answer every question. If asked about Regional or National level policies or issues, the spokesperson should politely refer the reporter to the Regional or National level media relations liaison, or the appropriate External Affairs Office. The spokesperson should assist to ensure the reporter makes contact with the appropriate Service spokesperson.

- All issues of high sensitivity or controversy should be discussed with Regional External Affairs Staff prior to making comments to news media representatives. Examples of sensitive and controversial issues include:
  — Accidents or incidents involving fatalities
  — Public criticism of Service, *especially from elected officials*
  — Personnel issues
  — Law Enforcement issues (Specific LE guidance has been issued in Service Manual at 443 FW 2)
  — Legal issues, such as lawsuits, etc.
  — Any management action that involves killing animals

- When appropriate during communications with news media reporters, the spokesperson should attempt to convey the Service's Basic Messages. (See Chapter 5).

- Press calls should be documented (Try using a Query Sheet — see this chapter) and a summary of press interactions should be reported weekly to the Regional Media Relations Liaison for possible inclusion in Regional Weekly reports to Washington (Call to check for your regional policies).

Who in your office is/are designated to serve as official Service spokesperson in response to calls from the press?

All persons designated to serve as official spokespersons are encouraged to take specialized training offered by the National Conservation and Training Center.

Characteristics of Key News Media

When dealing with reporters from each of the three news media types, keep in mind those special characteristics that will help you communicate specific types of information to various publics.

Newspapers:
- Can report in more detail than other media.

- Usually have more departments or sections, more specialty reporters for analytical stories.

- Deadlines are usually daily; cannot easily get first word on breaking news.

- Can take an editorial position; can include Guest Editorials.

- Features feedback in form of letters to editor.

- Usually will print corrections if their reports contain errors.

- Will consider using good quality photographs, graphs, charts, you provide.

- Require least logistics for reporters to cover stories (reporter, notebook).

- Usually only one daily newspaper per community

- Become historical record

Television:
- Emphasizes stories that are dynamic, sensational, and emotional.

- Stories are shorter, less detailed, less analytical than print media stories.

- Can report fast-breaking news several times per day.

- Little opportunity for corrections or feedback.

- Will often use good quality videotape you provide.

- Require most logistics to cover stories (reporter, photographer, sound technician, etc.)

- Usually several competing TV stations per community

- Very little difference in formats between competing TV stations

Radio:
- Reports in least detail

- Can report news fastest of all news media, usually on the hour.

- Many different formats (talk radio, all news, music with news, etc.)

- Different stations cater to different audiences

- Most accessible for public service announcements.

- Little opportunity for corrections or feedback.

- Requires little logistics (phone interviews, or reporter with tape recorder)

- Usually large number of radio stations per community

Do's and Don'ts for Interviews with News Media

Important Do's:
- Think through a basic single message. Use the opportunity to get it across.

- Include the Basic Service Messages.

- State important facts first.

- Repeat the messages in several ways.

- Bring the reporter back to YOUR point.

- Anticipate problem questions, and have responses ready for them all.

- Offer to put the reporter in touch with other knowledgeable contact people.

- Wear uniform or positive Service identification.

- If it is a TV interview, check your image in a mirror first.

- Offer to provide follow-up information

- Speak in public's interest, not agency's.

- Give a direct answer to a direct question.

- If you don't know the answer, say, "I can get you that information."

- Always tell the truth.

- Correct reporters when they make a mistake. Contact them immediately.

- Consult with Regional External Affairs Office.

Important Don'ts:
- Don't let a reporter put words in your mouth

- Don't make any statement that you don't want quoted, or speak "off the record."

- Don't argue or lose your cool

- Don't say "No comment," or "Because it's our policy."

- Don't ask to read or see a reporter's story prior to publication

- Don't use the news media to criticize others.

How to Build and Maintain Good Media Relations

Four Steps to Good News Media Relations:
Identity—Be sure the reporters likely to cover Service activities and issues know who you are. Call them and introduce yourself. Offer a tour of your facilities or a briefing on your activities. Be sure they understand your expertise and that of your staff members. Do not wait for a crisis.

Credibility—Be sure the reporters know your credentials, your background and your responsibilities. They will rely on you as a "source"—an expert spokesperson who can provide information on specific topics. Never risk your credibility by guessing, exaggerating, or faking it.

Reliability—Once you have established yourself as a source, be sure to be available for short-notice interviews. Always return calls promptly. Be proactive to bring issues of importance to the reporter's attention, both formally and informally.

Respect—Always remember that a reporter has a job to do. They have an ethic to be truthful and impartial. They have a role guaranteed by the First Amendment of the Constitution to be a government watchdog, and they take their job as seriously as you take yours.

Don't expect a good reporter to always treat you like a friend, but if your goal is for the American public to better understand who the Service is, what the Service does, and why the Service does it, then you share a lot of common ground with that reporter!

Pitching Stories to the Press

When bringing a story idea to a reporter, either in a news release or phone call, think in terms of the basic elements of a news story, and a story angle.

Story Elements:
Change—The definition of a news story is that it is something new, or previously unknown by the public. Focus on what is different. It could be a new way of doing things, or new information. For example, survey results and other studies often are sources of new information. Superlatives that come from records (best, worst, most, etc.) all are potential sources of news. Before you contact the reporter, decide:

- *What is the HEADLINE for this story?* Help the reporter get that headline.

Image—News stories are enhanced with an image. For newspapers or TV news, the image is a still photo or video. For radio, the image is conveyed by sound. Before you contact the reporter, decide:

- *What is the IMAGE that captures this story?* Help the reporter get that image.

Attitude—Most stories include a quote that gives a reaction from someone involved, a witness, a victim, or an expert on the subject matter. The reaction conveys emotion, context, or perspective in a sound bite. Before you contact the reporter, decide:

- *What will you say when quoted in this story?* Help the reporter to get your quote.

Story Angles:
- *Crime*—Abominable acts, abuse of power, law enforcement

- *Pocketbook issues/Economic Impacts*—Jobs, construction, tourism, Government saving or wasting money

- *The following topics offer good possibilities for wildlife stories:*

- *Good News/Bad News*—Survey results, threats to wildlife, listing actions.

- *Kids*—Learning about animals, helping animals

- *Help Wanted*—Asking public for help in finding criminals, report sightings, etc.

- *Spin-offs*—Wildlife links with other stories (droughts, fires, weather), and seasonal topics

- *Animal Stories*—Unusual behavior of animals, amusing photography, etc.

Writing a Press Release

General Principles:

1. A press release is an official expression of the Service that could reach thousands or even millions of people. Be sure it is totally accurate, and that it meets regional requirements for review prior to distribution (If you are unsure, check with your Regional Media Relations Liaison).

2. Use official Service letterhead, or designated Press Release form, which includes agency name and phone number and designated individual for follow up contacts.

3. It is NOT like scientific writing with key information and conclusions at the end. It should use active-voice prose, and begin with the most important message up front.

4. Include the appropriate Basic Service Messages.

5. The purpose of a press release is to generate responses from reporters that will lead to stories in the press, so be sure there will be someone available to respond immediately to questions from reporters.

When crafting your press release:

1. Before you begin, identify the objective for the press release, and develop the key message points you need to include.

2. Focus on the interests of the public: How are they affected? Why should they care?

3. Use inverted pyramid format, with most important facts at beginning and additional details in order of importance.

4. Construct a lead paragraph that answers the questions, "Who, what, when, where, why?" Sometimes you may need to discuss the "how."

5. Keep it simple, brief, and to the point.

6. Avoid jargon and acronyms.

7. Consider including a quote from a Service employee to help establish the Service's stake and credibility in the issue.

Correcting Mistakes

Reporters are human, and even after your best outreach efforts they sometimes make mistakes. After you have worked with a reporter on a story, be sure to read, watch, or listen to it carefully for any errors. Using tact and discretion, bring any errors immediately to the attention of the reporter. Keep in mind that they have a keen interest in getting facts correct if they are to survive in the information business, and errors are usually honest mistakes. They will not always be able or willing to make corrections, but your complaints will let them know they are under your scrutiny, and they will be more careful with Service stories in the future. *Whenever you see errors in media reports, advise your Regional Media Relations Liaison, specified Outreach Coordinator, or other External Affairs staff of the errors, and how you are responding.* They will alert other service offices and partners, as appropriate.

Correcting Errors in Broadcast Media:

1. When you see or hear an error, call the station and ask to speak to the reporter or someone on the news staff IMMEDIATELY to point out the error. Your early call may prevent the mistake from being repeated in a later newscast.

2. Your first call should always be to the reporter who made the error, if possible. If they convince you it was an honest error, you may want to let it drop.

3. If same reporter makes repeated errors, or seems to be biased toward making the Service look bad, contact the news director or station manager and inform them of the errors. Ask to have another reporter assigned to cover Service issues. Consult your Regional External Affairs office before taking this step.

Correcting Errors in Print Media:

1. When you see the error, call the reporter IMMEDIATELY to point out the error. Your early call may prevent the mistake from being repeated in later editions or syndication. Ask if the story may be picked up by a wire service (AP, UP, Reuters, etc.), and if so, ask for assistance to correct their versions.

2. Your first call should always be to the reporter who made the error, if possible. If they convince you it was an honest error and the error is relatively insignificant, you may want to let it drop. If it is a significant error, ask for a printed correction.

3. If same reporter makes repeated errors, or seems to be biased toward making the Service look bad, contact the editor and inform him/her of the errors. Ask to have another reporter assigned to cover Service issues. Consult your Regional External Affairs office before taking this step.

4. If you determine that the error requires a response in a letter to the editor, consult with your Regional Media Relations Liaison for guidance and assistance.

For guidance on writing Letters to the Editor and Op-Ed Pieces, see Appendix A-5

All persons who interact with news media are encouraged to take advantage of specialized training offered by the National Conservation and Training Center (NCTC).

Chapter 3.c.: Membership in Professional and Community Organizations

Summary: Service policies encourage employees to join professional organizations and community organizations to enhance Service professionalism and support. If approved in advance, Service funding may be available for designated membership activities.

A Critical Public: Non-Service Professional Peers

In difficult and controversial natural resource management issues, the Service can generate needed support with a variety of publics by gaining the support of non-Service professional peers. Their third-party endorsement of a Service position enhances Service credibility, helps build trust in the Service position, and helps move toward greater acceptance of the position by other publics.

One way for the Service to foster relationships with non-Service professional peers is for Service employees to become personally involved with professional organizations. When Service employees become members and participate in these organizations, they can enhance their own skills and capabilities while helping build visibility and respect for the Service.

See Director's Memorandum on pages 29-30 for complete details.

Membership in Community Organizations

By joining local community organizations, Service employees build bridges of trust with members of publics with whom they do not share the same professional interests. Instead, community organizations provide opportunities to build relationships based on informal communications regarding other, non-professional common interests, ranging from leisure activities to general community service. These informal communications become especially important for conveying credible information in a more neutral atmosphere on controversial issues.

See Director's Order No. 95 on pages 31-32 for complete details.

July 27, 1999

To: Fish and Wildlife Service Employees

From: Acting Director /s/ John G. Rogers

Subject: Membership and Participation in Professional Societies

To effectively serve the public in carrying out the U.S. Fish and Wildlife Service mission, we must maintain a diverse and highly qualified work force of professionals so that our management is based on the best available science and meets professional standards.

In recent years there have been many advances in knowledge of basic ecosystem processes, condition of public land resources, and management principles. With the many resource conservation challenges we face it is essential for all Service employees, regardless of occupation, to maintain and enhance their knowledge and skills.

We believe that membership, involvement, and participation in professional societies are more important now than ever, for the purposes of maintaining and enhancing our capabilities in professional resource management. Our membership and participation will not only help in developing a professional work force but also enhance the public perception of Service employees. Other intangible benefits associated with professional society involvement include:

> Higher agency visibility and enhanced reputation or respect through employee professional interactions, participation and networking with others;

> Employee growth in both ability and knowledge;

> Enhanced effectiveness of employees in carrying out Service programs;

> Enhanced employee morale, self-esteem and motivation; and

> Development of leadership qualities in Service employees.

Employees may serve in professional organizations under three different circumstances:

(A) The employee participates in the outside organization in his or her private capacity and not on Government time.

(B) The employee participates in the outside organization in his or her private capacity. However, the supervisor allows official time for the employee to attend an outside function of the association, such as a meeting or convention, when the supervisor determines that it is in the best interest of the Government, and does not result in a direct conflict of interest or create the appearance thereof.

(C) The Service requires that the employee participate in the outside organization in his or her official capacity, as a representative of the Service.

All employees who are required or who wish to serve as an officer in a private sector organization while on official Government duty time must (a) have a written Memorandum of Understanding between the Service and the organization in which the employee is required or desires to serve as an officer; (b) have a waiver of the conflict of interest prohibition at 18 U.S.C. 208(b) signed by the Service Deputy Ethics Counselor; and (c) secure training from the appropriate Ethics Counselor (See Director Order No. 117, dated December 22, 1998, for detailed information).

It is Service policy to support and encourage attendance at appropriate professional society meetings, while recognizing that budgetary constraints may limit the Service travel support for attending meetings. With this in mind, we need to review requests for attending non-governmental meetings on a case-by-case basis. When attendance is approved, the Service will assist with the travel expenses, attendance fees, and/or duty time for employee attendance at meetings. Where employees have personally paid membership dues and contributed personal time and money to maintain professional status, managers should give priority consideration for attendance at meetings.

We recognize that the Service has limited budgetary resources to pay travel and attendance fees for everyone who wants to attend a non-governmental meeting. We must set criteria for determining who the Service will assist in attending the meeting of societies, organizations, or associations. Criteria listed in priority ranking are offered below to help in determining attendance at non-governmental meetings for the following:

1. Officials or committee chairpersons in the sponsoring organization, association or society; or,

2. Presenters of papers, speeches or instructors as part of the official program; or,

3. Service representatives who are a spokesperson or on official duties that require interfacing with the organization; or,

4. Employees with previously identified training needs as reflected in an Individual Development Plan to enhance their job performance which would be provided by attending symposiums, paper sessions, or continuing education training at the scheduled meeting; or,

5. General members of the sponsoring organization.

In closing, all managers should encourage professional affiliation and membership in appropriate organizations, associations, and societies. Managers should take opportunities to invite members from professional organizations to discuss their activities with employees and to involve Service representatives in outside task groups or steering committees.

United States Department of the Interior
FISH AND WILDLIFE SERVICE
Washington, D.C. 20240

DIRECTOR'S ORDER NO. 95
Subject: Membership in Community Organizations

Sec. 1 Purpose. This Order promulgates revised U.S. Fish and Wildlife Service policy concerning Service and employee membership in community organizations.

Sec. 2 Scope. This policy applies to all Service offices and employees. Community organizations included under this policy are those such as the Lion's Club, the Kiwanis Club, chambers of commerce, or similar organizations that are established to further community well being and whose purpose and objectives are consistent with those of the Service. Membership in political and professional organizations is addressed elsewhere and is excluded from the scope of this Order.

Sec. 3 Policy.

1. Service employees may join any community organization provided that such membership is paid for by the individual, is for the individual, and does not in any way imply membership as an employee of the Service. As members of community organizations, all views must be expressed as those of the individual and not as those of the Service. Employees who pay their own membership dues may not lawfully represent the organization before a Federal agency, except in limited circumstances. Questions regarding a specific representation situation should be directed to the appropriate servicing ethics counselor.

2. Where a Regional Director or Assistant Director determines it is in the best interest of the Service and where such action will promote outreach to members of the local community and encourage better understanding and cooperation, he or she may authorize the use of appropriated funds to secure Service membership in community organizations included within the scope of this Order.

   (1) This determination will be made on a case-by-case basis. This authority may not be re-delegated. The membership must be established in the name of the Service. Appropriated funds are not to be used to establish memberships in the name of any individual although a Service employee or employees may be designated to represent the Service at meetings and functions of the community organization. Any individual representing the Service is expected to maintain the position of the Service with regard to representing the organization before any Federal agency or any other entity.

3. Service employees are prohibited from serving in an official capacity as officer, director, trustee, or employee of a community organization. The U.S. Department of Justice recently issued an opinion that states that serving in an official capacity as an officer, director, or trustee in a non-federal, non-profit entity is a violation of 18 U.S.C. 208, a criminal statute. The Department of the Interior, Office of the Solicitor, is currently reviewing this issue. It is expected that the Department will issue policy requiring employees to obtain a statutory waiver in order to serve in an official capacity as an officer in an outside organization. We will issue Service policy once guidance is received from the Department.

4. Where an individual membership in a community organization is established under section 3a, an individual serving as an officer, director, trustee, or employee of the community organization must recuse himself/herself from working on any particular matter as a government employee when the organization in which he or she is serving has a financial interest in those government matters.

5. Where an employee joins a community organization under section 3a, it is very unlikely that the government would provide legal representation to the employee in the event a law suit is filed against the community organization or the employee as the result of the employee's activities with the community organization. Even where the employee is a Service representative under section 3b, a case-by-case determination regarding government legal representation will have to be made.

Sec. 4 Effective Date. This order is effective immediately and will remain in effect until incorporated in the Fish and Wildlife Service Manual or until it is amended, superseded, or revoked, whichever occurs first. In the absence of the foregoing actions, the provisions of this Order will terminate and be considered obsolete on December 31, 1997.

SGD/ JOHN G. ROGERS
Acting Director

Date: May 14, 1997

_____ (note: effective date has been extended.)

1. To be an eligible organization for Service membership, the community organization may not discriminate in membership on the basis of any reason such as race, sex, religion, age, national origin, disability, or sexual orientation.

Chapter 4: Special Outreach Tools

Chapter 4.a.: Environmental Education:
It's Not Just Kid Stuff

Environmental Education — Definition

"Education" is gaining knowledge, understanding, and skills, by study, instruction, or experience. "Environmental education" (EE) is gaining knowledge, understanding, skills, and experience about the environment (i.e. wildlife and ecosystems) through study, instruction or experience.

Environmental education, when planned to support our goals and objectives for resource management, can be a powerful outreach tool. Environmental education is a process aimed at developing a world population that is aware of and concerned about the total environment, and its associated problems. It provides the knowledge, skills, attitudes, motivation, and commitment to work individually and collectively toward solutions for current problems and the prevention of new ones.

EE has been referred to as "a long-term means to the even longer-term end." Many educators have recognized the long-term advantage of reaching out to young people who are still forming the values they will hold throughout their life times. As such, they are much more receptive to new ideas than their adult counterparts and far more likely to adopt a philosophy of natural resource conservation that will stay with them throughout their lives.

Broadening the Scope of Environmental Education:
Does EE need to be limited to young people? Absolutely not. For one thing, EE programs can become a bridge for working with other publics, such as public interest groups and community organizations working toward goals they have in common with the Service. In addition, the creative approaches to learning that EE programs often use

can be adopted for use with other publics in non-academic forums, such as presentations to groups, special events, and even one-on-one meetings with opinion leaders.

To be effective, EE cannot stand alone to carry messages to all publics. The 1998 survey data from the National Report Card on Environmental Knowledge, Attitudes, and Behaviors found "no evidence that parents have higher levels of environmental knowledge than other adults," so we can not do just "kids" programs as a way of reaching adults. Though it can be a powerful force for outreach, EE must be a part of a well coordinated, comprehensive outreach plan that uses the best tools to convey the same basic message, adjusted for each separate audience.

To keep pace with the increasing complexity of resource-management issues, Service-conducted EE is broadening its scope to reach beyond the formal education setting with K-12 audiences to education of target audiences of all ages. This does not mean that we stop working with children, but that we consider them as one of many audiences to reach. From the day we are born until the day we die, we all continue to learn. As our experiences change, and knowledge and awareness are enhanced, our attitudes and behaviors shift accordingly. Service EE strives to recognize that all publics are subject to continuing education and works toward behavior shifts being responsible towards the environment.

Many excellent EE plans and materials have already been developed. Before you spend time or resources on curriculum development, check out what may be available from fellow Service EE specialists and nationally recognized EE organizations. Ask your Assistant Regional Director,

External Affairs, or check with the National Conservation Training Center for assistance.

Part of the Plan:
EE benefits the Service most when it is part of a larger National Outreach Strategy, with its goals, audiences, and messages. When developing educational materials, be sure they complement the Strategy and other Service outreach plans, with complementary goals, target audiences, and specific messages that need to reach those audiences.

As Service Director Jamie Rappaport Clark has said, "I urge you to think about environmental education in new ways; not just as kid stuff, but as a way to reach additional audiences and build new community partnerships in support of healthy fish, wildlife, and plant resources for the future."

Guidelines for Environmental Education in Outreach

According to the *National Outreach Strategy*, environmental education activities should be planned and executed and support other Service outreach to:

1. Include information about the Service and its mission (Basic Messages).

2. Help build community relationships.

3. Support specific Service resource priorities.

4. Make effective use of Service resources.

5. Serve the needs of field stations.

6. Reach the broadest possible audience.

When effectively integrated into Service outreach plans, EE can help in these ways:

1. Reach other influential members of the community, including teachers, school board members, and elected officials.

2. Enlist the help of young people in projects that benefit resources, such as environmental clean-up, visitor services, and monitoring wildlife activities (for example, the Internet-based Sister Schools Shorebird Project)

3. Generate opportunities for news media coverage.

4. Build a long-term constituency of individuals who value the nation's fish and wildlife resources.

Guiding Principles for Environmental Education:

1. Environmental education is an important and effective management tool and should be resource-based to meet the Service mission and management goals and objectives.

2. Environmental education services should be multi-disciplinary and multi-cultural to meet the needs of all populations.

3. Environmental education should aim to develop in people of all ages an understanding, appreciation, and support for fish and wildlife management and encourage active participation in resource protection.

Outcomes:

A sense of ownership in the fish and wildlife related issues of the local area will generate a sense of concern and support for fish and wildlife management policies and national programs. Environmental education programs developed and implemented within the Service must meet nationally established criteria, yet be tailored to meet each Region's needs and issues. Model programs, curriculum packages, teacher training workshops, and other programs will enable participants to:

1. Gain an appreciation for the importance of fish and wildlife resources and their habitats

2. Understand the ecological concepts upon which Service management concepts are based.

3. Comprehend the issues surrounding the management of fish and wildlife resources, and the critical problems confronting the resources.

4. Make informed, responsible decisions about fish and wildlife resources and take positive action toward solving the problems confronting the resources.

Community-Based Education:

One powerful and effective environmental education strategy is community-based education. This strategy involves conducting the outreach in the area where change needs to occur, and specifically aiming for the different age groups or constituents within that area. A typical community-based approach might include the following:

- Conducting a teacher workshop

- K-12 (kindergarten through twelfth grade) education activities at the school

- Hosting a family evening or weekend program or presentation,

- Hosting a city meeting,

- Providing an open house, and

- Having a meal or coffee break with key individuals in the community.

Success hinges on reaching everyone in the community in some way during the same time frame. Eventually, citizens of all ages throughout the community will recognize the consistency of the messages you want to convey through your education programs. When they begin to discuss the issue among themselves, the program is working!

In large cities, where a sense of community may be lost, proper front-end outreach planning will help ensure the correct "outreach mix" to needed to bolster the education component and increase chances of success. The broad reach of community-based environmental education greatly enhances its ability to support resource management objectives.

Do's and Don'ts for Successful Environmental Education Programs

Important Do's:
- Plan your environmental education programs to directly reflect your resource management issues.

- Plan your K-12 education curriculum to meet the National Science Standards.

- When possible, take a community-based approach to environmental education.

- Make your programs fun and engaging (hands-on learning).

- Focus on your specific messages, goals, and objectives.

- Evaluate the success of your programs frequently.

- Consider education programs for all ages.

- Be flexible and creative.

Important Don'ts:
- Don't lose sight of your goal because it seems to be taking too long to get there. Baby steps are okay!

- Don't forget to provide opportunities for people to get involved in conservation initiatives.

- Don't get stuck in a rut. If one method isn't working, just restructure your program.

- Don't hesitate to reach out to your colleagues and friends for ideas and support.

- Don't do programs that are not working towards your management and education goals and objectives.

- Don't forget that you are a role model to students and other people, on or off the job.

- Don't forget to reward your partners/volunteers for their support.

- Don't say "I can't afford it" or "I don't have time." We can't afford to NOT do education.

- Don't rely on environmental education alone to communicate about immediate issues. EE is a long term effort and only one part of an effective outreach program.

Persons involved in environmental education are encouraged to take advantage of specialized training offered by the National Conservation and Training Center (NCTC).

Key Contacts for Environmental Education

Service Contacts:

This Office:
Environmental Education Point of Contact: _____

Regional Office:
Environmental Education Point of Contact: _____ Phone/Fax _____ E-mail _____

Other Regional Points of Contact: _____ Phone/Fax _____ E-mail _____

National Conservation
Training Center:
Points of Contact: _____ Phone/Fax _____ E-mail _____

Area School Contacts:

School: _____ Address: _____

Environmental Education Point of Contact: _____

Phone/Fax _____ E-mail _____ Comments: _____

School: _____ Address: _____

Environmental Education Point of Contact: _____

Phone/Fax _____ E-mail _____ Comments: _____

School: _____ Address: _____

Environmental Education Point of Contact: _____

Phone/Fax _____ E-mail _____ Comments: _____

School: _____ Address: _____

Environmental Education Point of Contact: _____

Phone/Fax _____ E-mail _____ Comments: _____

Chapter 4.b.: The Internet/Intranet and Listservers

Internet: As the number of people who are "online" increases, so does the importance of including the Internet in outreach planning as an important communications tool. When used skillfully, the Internet can relay information to the scientific community, the education community, other agencies, the business community, and many others.

As with any outreach tool, the Internet is most effective when used in concert with coordinated outreach involving traditional tools. You see articles and ads in newspapers, magazines, and on television and radio, highlighting Internet addresses (URLs). You see URLs on business cards. Web pages enhance standard outreach techniques, rather than replace them.

Each Region and many Service programs have websites already in place. If you are contemplating using the Internet for your outreach activity, get in touch with your Regional External Affairs Office and your Regional Webmaster for specific policies, guidance and advice.

Intranet (SII): The Service's Internal Internet, or the SII, operates like an Internet website but has been designed to be used and accessed only by Service employees. It allows us to store and share information not used by the general public, like meeting notes, procedures and policies, document drafts, discussions, etc. Visit the SII at http://sii.fws.gov.

Name/Number of Regional Webmaster:

_____

For general guidance, be sure to check out the Service's Web Publishing Home Page at http://sii.fws.gov/webpublish/ and the Outreach Home Page in the Service's Internal Intranet at http://sii.fws.gov/outreach/

Both are solid sources of additional, up-to-date information and who-to-contact links. For guidance on specific Internet/Intranet activities, check the dozens of Online Tutorials at http://sii.fws.gov/webpublish/train/tutorials.htm

Several of particular interest are:

- How to Plan and Coordinate Your Web Site With Others Inside/Outside FWS

- How to Choose the Right Tool (Print Publications, Web Pages, Listservers, Newsgroups, TV, etc.)

- How to Write for the Web Audience(s)

- How to Build and Maintain a Site With Non FWS Partners

- How FWS Can Advertise and Sell Products Via the Web

- How to Build a Virtual Visitor Center

The Service also has a publications site at http://www.nctc.fws.gov/library/.

Advantages of Internet in Outreach:

- Access to large numbers of the public, both nationally and internationally.

- Ability to target specific publics.

- Ability to measure effectiveness (number of "hits").

- Ability to obtain direct feedback from on-line public.

- Ability to include very complex information, including graphics, maps, etc.

- Rapid transfer of information (highly important in crises, controversies).

- Reduction of costs for printing and mailing publications and documents.

Web pages allow you to "broadcast" (and color pictures are free!) and they also allow you to "narrowcast." We can bypass the filtering done by the mass media. On the Web, you can reach biologists, farmers, schoolteachers, and other audiences with a tighter focus than even radio provides.

Disadvantages of Internet in Outreach:

- Requires expense, expertise, and time to build and maintain a useful website.

- May be subject to "hacking," viruses, or other information distortion.

- On-line Public is generally limited to middle or upper income population.

- For maximum exposure, websites generally require promotion by other means of communication.

The official Directorate guidance regarding Web publishing is online at: http://sii.fws.gov/webpublish/dirguide.htm

Director's Memo (May 28, 1998) creating the Web Publishing Council

Director's Memo (October 13, 1998) requiring Web publishing plans from each AD/RD and the actual Web Publishing Plans that resulted.

All Employee Message (October 19, 1998) on Coordination and Review of Service Internet Publications.

Listservers

The Service uses various web-based Listservers to broadcast simple and quick information to a list of internal and external subscribers. Listservers are another way of receiving up to date information which appears in you email. Those who are involved in outreach should consider subscribing to the fws-outreach listserver, along with the fws-news listserver and the fws-web listserver to stay up-to-speed on what's happening in Service outreach, news/press releases and web management.

To subscribe to the fws-outreach listserver:
Click on *New Memo*

In the "To:" brackets type,
`listserv@www.fws.gov`

Leave the "Subject:" line blank.

Tab into the body section of the message and type:
`subscribe fws-outreach`
`your email name`

Click on *Send*.

To subscribe to the fws-news listserver:
Go to http://news.fws.gov/listser.html

Chapter 4.c.: Partnerships

Forming partnerships can be the Service's most successful and productive outreach activity. By forming partnerships, the Service establishes the closest possible relationships with members of publics that are willing to provide the highest level of support for specific issues. Virtually all Service programs and initiatives can be strengthened through the formation of partnerships.

Partnerships—Definitions:

A partnership is a type of collaboration. Collaboration is a mutually beneficial and well-defined relationship entered into by two or more organizations to achieve results they are more likely to achieve together than alone.

A partnership is a voluntary collaboration of individuals, organizations, or both, to achieve common goals on a specific project within a definite amount of time. It often involves exchange or flow of money or resources.

Why Partnerships?
As many Service project leaders have recognized, partnerships often provide the only politically and fiscally practical way to resolve conflicts in an increasingly competitive and complex world. As they go through the process of forming these bonds with specific publics, the project leaders learn more about these publics, their concerns and their strengths. Once the bond of partnership is properly forged, both agency and public take on a "we're all in this together" attitude, and the resources are the beneficiaries.

Advantages of Partnerships to Service Outreach:

- The existence of a partnership conveys a high level of trust and confidence in the Service on a given issue, thereby enhancing Service credibility among other publics.

- Partners can assist the Service by helping to convey Service outreach messages to other publics.

- Partnerships strengthen Service programs and activities by contributing financial, intellectual, and/or moral support from partners.

- Partners bring the strength of diversity to an agency or project.

Partnership Assessment Guide

- Will the partnership solve or significantly impact a problem?

- Is the time available for participation by partners?

- Are the goals of the project in the interest of the agency and within its mandate?

- Do your prospective partners all have a reason to participate in the partnership?

- Are cooperation and collaboration needed to do the project?

- Do you need additional information or resources that the partners can provide?

- Is acceptance of the decision or project critical to effective implementation?

- If you made the decision or did the project on your own, would the involved stakeholders accept it?

- Has the partnership identified all groups needed for the project to be successful?

- Will the partnership be voluntary and equitable?

Do's and Don'ts of Partnerships

Do:
- Take the initiative. Talk to people. Think creatively about ways to work with others to achieve commons goals while furthering agency objectives.

- Clearly define the objectives of a potential partnership, the resources that each participant would bring to the activity, and the benefits that each stands to gain.

- Be inclusive. Early on, involve people whose approval or participation will be ultimately required.

- Put ideas in writing for people who may be interested. Make sure to represent them as ideas rather than agreement.

- Learn about prospective partners. Be comfortable with their reputations and capabilities before joining or forming a partnership with them.

- Investigate alternative strategies for achieving the objective. Are other avenues or other partners better suited to accomplish the objectives?

- Be realistic in estimating the often lengthy time periods required to initiate and implement a partnership. Anticipate, be prepared for, and expect delays.

Don't:
- Limit the ways you use partnerships to further agency objectives.

- Wait until the last minute to bring in supervisors, public affairs, or agreement specialists to review the contemplated partnership.

- Endorse any company or external product that will be put up for sale.

- Exceed your authority to solicit partnership funding from private sources.

- Lose focus on the goals of the partnerships.

- Get into turf battles.

- Get frustrated if there are delays. Remember that time periods are estimates only!

For additional information on forming partnerships, see Appendix A-6

All persons involved in forming partnerships are encouraged to take advantage of specialized training offered by the National Conservation and Training Center (NCTC).

Glossary of Outreach Terms

Above the Fold — Literally, the location on the front page of a newspaper that appears above where the newspaper is folded. This location is reserved for the most important stories.

Actuality — The portion of a radio news report which is recorded at the scene of the story, including natural sound or taped interview.

Ambush Interview — When a TV news crew arrives without advance notice to interview a person who is not expecting the interview. Caught off-guard, the subject of the interview often looks furtive or guilty of something.

Anchor — A news person who usually is broadcast from the TV station and introduces stories by other reporters, or reads stories from behind a desk. Often anchors work in pairs.

Angle — The approach, focus, or emphasis that a reporter takes when preparing a story.

Arbitron — A commonly used service which measures broadcast audiences for radio stations.

Art — In newspapers and magazines, and illustration, chart, graphic, or photograph that accompanies a story.

Assignment Editor — In a radio or TV newsroom, the person who determines which reporters and photographers will cover which stories. Though the assignment editor is not the only member of a news staff who determines which stories will be covered, he/she is the single best person to contact if you have a story you want to be covered.

B Roll — Videotape showing scenes or images that are generally related to a particular story or subject, such as scenery, wildlife, people working, etc. B roll is used during the editing process to add additional visual interest to a story.

Bird — A broadcast satellite.

Bite — Short for "sound bite," referring to the small portion of a recorded radio or TV interview which is used in the reporter's story. Bites usually last no more than 15 seconds. Bites from separate portions of the same interview may be edited together to make them appear as if they were spoken together.

Block — A set of news stories on a news cast which are broadcast together, without interruption for a commercial break. Stories in the first "block" are those the station deems most newsworthy.

Break — In TV: The periods of the newscast during which commercials are run. In Newspapers: The place where a story ends on one page, to be continued on another.

Breaking News — See "news" below. "Breaking" news is distinguished by that news which is most immediate, or happening at the time of the report.

Bug — A small microphone that can transmit conversations. A bug that is secretly planted to record conversations without the knowledge of those recorded is illegal under FCC regulations except when used by police with a warrant.

Bulldog Edition — The first edition of a newspaper.

Call Letters — The letters which identify radio and TV broadcast stations. Stations west of the Mississippi begin with "K," east of the Mississippi they begin with "W."

Canned Story, or In the Can — A story that is ready to be printed or broadcast. Often used to refer to a story written or produced by a wire service, network, or source other than the news organization using it.

Congress — For purposes of Service outreach, the term "Congress" encompasses members of the U.S. House of Representatives and the U.S. Senate, and members of their staffs, both in Washington D.C. and in their home states or districts.

Chroma-Key — A TV device used to superimpose graphics or words on the image being broadcast, such as the name and title of the person shown speaking.

Crawl — Additional information in the form of words and numbers which move horizontally across the bottom of the TV image while regular programming is underway. Usually provides emergency or bulletin information such as weather warnings, elections results, etc.

Cutline — The information below a photograph which describes the contents of the photograph and may give photo credit.

Dateline — The first words in a print news story which indicate where the story comes from, and often the source, which is often a wire service, for example, SAN FRANCISCO — Reuters. In prior years, the date was also included (hence the name "dateline"), but today all news stories are assumed to be dated the same day as published, and most papers delete the date.

Defamation—"Communication that exposes a person to hatred, ridicule, or contempt, or lowers him in the esteem of his fellows, causes him to be shunned, or injures his business or calling. Its categories are libel–broadly, printed or written material; and slander–broadly, spoken words." (–Law of Mass Communications, *Nelson and Teeter.*)

DBS—Direct broadcast satellite, referring to a satellite which relays TV signals directly to the viewer from the source, rather than to a local TV station or cable system for relay to the viewer.

Display Advertising—Newspaper ads that use large blocks of space, usually including art or photos, distinguished from classified ads.

Dub—Copy of a videotape or audio tape.

ENG—Electronic news gathering using videotape as the medium.

Environmental Education (EE)— Gaining knowledge, understanding, skills, and experience about the environment (i.e. wildlife and habitats) through study, instruction or experience.

Equal Time—The federal requirement that any broadcast station which provides air time to a political candidate during the election process must provide equal time to other candidates.

Exclusive—A news story that only one news outlet covers, sometimes by arrangement with the source of the story. Also called a "scoop."

Fairness Doctrine—In the past, this was a federal FCC requirement that broadcasters cover all sides of controversial stories of public importance. This requirement was repealed in 1987.

FCC—The Federal Communications Commission, which regulates all electronic transmissions in the U.S., including radio, TV, cell phones, etc.

Feature—A news story that may not be as timely or urgent as "hard" news, and usually has a human interest angle.

Grip—An assistant who works with a TV crew, usually the sound technician.

Hard News—See "News," below. "Hard" news is distinguished by its emphasis on facts—the who, what, where, when, and how of the story— with a minimum of interpretation.

Hot—In broadcast production, any of the following: a microphone that is on; sound that is too loud; lighting that is too bright.

Intercut—A TV editing technique that places one person's interview directly next to another person's interview, without showing the reporter, usually to heighten controversy between opposing viewpoints.

Key Informant—An individual member of a particular public or group whom you can rely on to help you understand what that group is thinking or feeling about particular issue.

Kicker—The last story in a newscast, usually something cute, funny, or unusual, to end the newscast on an upbeat note.

Lead—The opening sentence or paragraph of a print news story, which usually contains addresses the who, what, where, when of the story.

Lead-In—The part of a news story read by the anchor to introduce the reporter's story. The broadcast equivalent of the headline for the story.

Libel—See "Defamation," above.

Listener—A video shot of the reporter listening the to the person being interviewed. Sometimes called "noddies," because the reporters often nod during the shot, as if they agree with or understand what the person is saying. These shots are used in the editing process as cutaways for smoother transitions between sound bites.

Masthead—The box in a newspaper that shows the newspaper name, editor, publisher, often on the editorial page.

Morgue—The library of a newspaper that keeps copies of previous stories by subject. Reporters rely on morgues for background information.

News—A timely event that will have wide interest to most people, such as a disaster, an important discovery, unusual weather event, etc. Generally, the news media consider an event to be "news" if they say it is.

News Director—The person in charge of the entire news department in a TV or radio station, and who does the hiring and firing of all reporters, anchors and technical crew.

News Hole—The space in a newspaper for news stories, which increases or decreases along with the amount of the advertising for the day.

News Peg—A local news story that is linked to another larger or ongoing story, including national or international stories.

Op-Ed—The page in a newspaper opposite the editorial page, which usually contains other opinions, letters to the editor, etc.

Out-Takes—Audio and videotape taken in the course of news gathering, but not used in the story that is aired.

Outreach—Two-way communication between the U.S. Fish and Wildlife Service and the public to establish mutual understanding, promote involvement, and influence attitudes and actions, with the goal of improving joint stewardship of our natural resources.

Package—A complete videotape production of an individual TV news story, which usually includes the reporters report, background audio and video, and one or more interviews.

Partnership—Voluntary collaboration of individuals, organizations, or both, to achieve common goals on a specific project within a definite amount of time. It often involves exchange or flow of money or resources.

Pool—A group of reporters and photographers who agree among themselves that one will cover the story and share the story and/or photos/video with others. These arrangements are usually made only when access to a story location is limited. *Note: If a government official can offer only limited access to a story location (for instance, because space on an aircraft is limited), the official should allow interested reporters to make their own pool arrangements, not assign one.*

PSA—Public Service Announcement. Used on radio and TV stations like commercials, these short spots generally run free of charge, from 10 to 60 seconds each, and address some item of general public interest. Though no longer required by FCC regulations, most stations still run PSAs to meet their general FCC licensing requirement to operate "in the public interest."

Reader—A story that is read by an anchor news person, without accompanying visuals.

Release—A written agreement that gives permission for the media to use one's picture or voice for commercial purposes. A release is not needed for news coverage.

Scoop—See "Exclusive" above.

Second Generation—Videotape image copied from the original videotape. With each successive copy of a copy (third generation, fourth, etc.), the image quality deteriorates rapidly.

Side Bar—A secondary story related to a larger story. Side Bars are often feature story treatments of an element from a hard news story.

Slander—See "Defamation," above.

Standup—The portion of a TV news story in which the reporter is shown speaking directly to the viewer, usually from the location, and to close the story.

Talent—Jargon for those in TV news who are actually shown on TV, i.e., the reporters, anchors, weather forecasters, and not the photographers, technicians, etc.

Tight Shot—A picture in which only one person is shown, often a closeup of the person's face, with little visible background.

Tombstone—Two newspaper story headlines are placed side-by-side, with similar type size and font, so readers may confuse them as one continuous headline. It is a bad layout.

Two-Shot—A picture showing two persons, usually the reporter and the interview subject talking together.

Wrap—A TV or radio story that is "wrapped" around a quote from someone being interviewed. See also, "Package" above. The term is also used to indicate a scene or production is satisfactory and is concluded, as in "That's a wrap."